NEUROSCIENCE AND COGNITIVE PSYCHOLOGY IN REVOLUTIONAIZING THE CRIMINAL JUSTICE SYSTEM IN INDIA

VOLUME 2, ISSUE 3 OF BRILLOPEDIA

PALAK GUPTA

Contents

Preface

"Start writing, no matter what. The water does not flow until the faucet is turned on".

• Louis L'Amour

Hundreds of students and professors are contributing their work to Brillopedia, we are here to provide ample information about Law and Contemporary issues. Our aim is to provide a platform for today's generation to express their views and ideas on law and contemporary law.

Author

Author is a **Paralegal serving for U.S. Supreme Court and is practicing Advocate before Supreme Court of India, Bombay High Court, Delhi High Court and Punjab and Haryana High Court.** Author completed her education in **BSc. (Medical)** from Government PG College AmbalaCantt hence, moving to Mumbai to pursue her dream of doing Law. She completed her **LLB and LLM** from University of Mumbai. She was topper of her batches throughout all her education. She has been *thrice awarded by Chief Justice of India, Chief Minister of State, Educational Minister and Chief Justice of various High Courts.* She won various National and International competitions in Moot Courts, debate, elocution, declamation, Acting and Kick Boxing tournaments. She served as Secretary General of College and got felicitate as best student. Author has worked with many big shot advocates such as *Soli Sorabjee, MukulRohtagi, RaahulTrivedi, Ashok R. Trivedi, Justice Vinod Prasad, AOR Prabodh Kumar,MahalaxmiPavani, Justice Vimlesh, Vijesh Sharma (Deputy Adv. General Punjab and Haryana High Court), RK Gupta (Deputy Advocate General) Punjab and Haryana High Court.* She has argued in various matters of **NDPS, Prostitution, Gang Rape** before eminent Supreme Court Judges such as **J. DY Chandrachud, J.**

InduMalhotra etc. and victoriously got matters in her favour at a small age before Supreme Court. Recently assisted the New York Court with matter pertaining to Bob Marley and his children.As a writer she wrote a book- *"World Destined her with correct soul"*and her next book is in process which recently got pre launched. Her upcoming book is *Men with Dreams v. Women with dreams.*She got her first Research Paper published with title –*"three fold comparative analysis of rape laws in terms of heteronormativity, marital rape and corrective rape".* She has more than 3 years of experience in handling the matters before Hon'ble Supreme Court and also worked with reputed Real Estate Companies, Cyber Lawyers, Criminal Lawyers, Law firms at different positions and levels.

Publication

This research paper is published in volume 2, issue 3 of Brillopedia

CHAPTER ONE

ABSTRACT

In the field of occupational science, cognitive neuroscience is emerging as a sales trend, especially in the area of workplace evaluation and statistics. In spite of this, occupational applications have not traditionally been a major emphasis of the discipline, which has instead primarily been concerned with the therapeutic and academic significance of its research. We will investigate three emerging areas where cognitive neuroscience research techniques and theory are producing practical workplace benefits. [1]Given that many in the field of brain research are probably unfamiliar with this application, we want to describe notions that should be regarded as crucial considerations when applying novel methods to the workplace. In light of these essential factors, a number of obstacles prevent cognitive neuroscience from becoming more than a passing fad in the field of occupational research.

Submission of this Research Paper is an author's initiative to link the disciplines of Cognitive Psychology and Neuroscience with present Criminal legal and justice system in India with a suggestive approach towards a distinctive niche of making India technologically upgraded in positive manner so that science and technology proves to be a boon to criminal justice system and its victims rather being an enterprise ill-suited to law.A pragmatic focus by the Author has been made on the fact that how highly qualified brains and disciplines of science can enhance and change the face of Criminal Justice System as well as its administration. This Research Paper is an integration of three disciplines to bring out new revolution in the approach of looking ahead to Artificial intelligence and sciences as an effective contributory to the Indian Legal System.

[1] COGNITIVE NEUROSCIENCE AND PSYCHOTHERAPY Available at-https://www.sciencedirect.com/topics/psychology/cognitive-neuroscience (Last accessed on 20.10.2022 at 11:30 PM).

CHAPTER TWO

BACKGROUND

The study of how mental processes originate from the brain's underlying electrical and chemical activity is known as cognitive neuroscience. Patterns of neuronal activity serve as active representations in the brain, information is processed as it is carried through excitatory and inhibitory connections, and learning and memory emerge as a result of rewiring the network. Some researchers have proposed that different brain areas perform separate, contained processing tasks, while others have proposed that each region contributes in a unique manner to a distributed, interactive process.[1]

The study of lesions on cognitive functions in humans and animals, single- and multi-electrode recordings of neuronal activity during cognitive processes, studies of human functional brain activity using non-invasive methods like fMRI and PET, and the use of computational models to formalise explicit hypotheses about the underlying mechanisms all contribute to the field. Some of these approaches first appeared in the '80s and '90s, and they are just going to become better and more widespread in the years to come. There will undoubtedly be more advances in our knowledge of the neurological foundation of cognition because of this. The goal of cognitive neuroscience is to better understand the mind by applying findings from neuroscientific research to the problem. How do the neuronal chemical and electrical impulses give birth to cognitive functions like perception, memory, comprehension, insight, and reasoning? How is the physical structure of the brain utilised to store, retrieve, and apply information (including knowledge of the external world, one's own past, and honed skills like language and performance)? These are some of the most fundamental concerns that cognitive neuroscience seeks to answer.[2]

[1] J.L. McClelland-"*Cognitive Neuroscience*", International Encyclopedia of Social and Behavourial Sciences (2001).

[2] Ibid.

CHAPTER THREE

INTRODUCTION

The growing use of neuroscience in legal situations has warranted a critical discussion of the extent to which it may be used. Some extreme perspectives have been taken in high-profile arguments, either dismissing or exaggerating the importance that neuroscience plays in assessing legal liability. In this article, we take a conciliatory stance by reiterating the importance of neurobiology in law and discussing its impact on changing public perceptions of criminal responsibility. Taking a middle ground on the debate over how science and the law interact allows for more constructive examination of real-world reforms that might enhance our legal decision-making. Neuroscience offers a promising new avenue for exploring the complex causes of antisocial conduct. At the end of the day, we argue that the changing normative views regarding culpability in light of developing neuroscience are unlikely to lead to significant reforms in the way we allocate legal blame. Instead, it encourages us to let go of our worst retributivist impulses in favour of more realistic approaches to addressing the most glaring causes of mass imprisonment and recidivism.

CHAPTER FOUR

CONCEPT AND TERMINOLOGY

As per the definition of Merriam Webster, Neuroscience[1] "is *the study of the nervous system and its role in behaviour and learning, including its structure and function at the cellular, biochemical, and molecular levels.*"[2]Neuroscience is nothing but a multidisciplinary branch of biology that is an amalgamation of anatomy, physiology, cytology, molecular biology, developmental biology, mathematical modelling, computer science, psychology and engineering. It has been stated as an *"Ultimate Challenge to Biology in 21st century".*

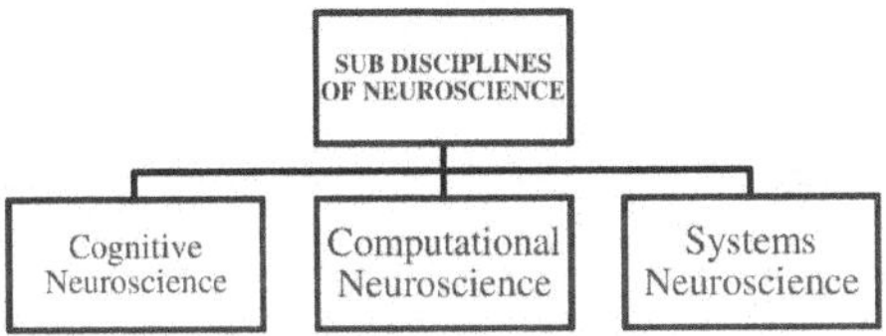

Therefore, neuroscience and neuroscientists[1]primarily have their focus on brain, its functioning and impact of brain on people, their psychology and behavior. Brain being the most important part of human body performs the crucial role in building the psychology of a criminal and a victim. In the **Criminal Jurisprudence, Penal Codes and Criminal Justice System**, Rule of ***Mens Rea*** i.e. *Guilty mind* has been placed before ***Actus Reus*** i.e. Wrongful act. Therefore, to constitute an offence, a wrongful act must be accompanied by a guilty mind. Therefore, Neuroscience and neuropsychology is a way to easily discover that guilty mind.Apart from its utility of providing useful insights and finding out a murderer from brain imaging technique or by identifying the genes of psychopathy, it can also be used further to strengthen the diagnosis of 'Shaken Baby Syndrome' or 'Non Accidental Head Injury'. Cognitive psychology is also the study of mind as an information processor but, the fruitful efforts of cognitive psychologists try to build the models of information processing to go inside the human brain and deliver the conclusion on the basis of perception, attention, memory, thinking, language and consciousness.

[1] Greene and Cohen 2004 For the law, neuroscience changes nothing and everything. Philosophical Transactions of the Royal Society B 359, 1775–1785.

[1] NEUROSCIENCE AND THE LAW: BRAIN, MIND, AND THE SCALES OF JUSTICE 206 (Brent Garland ed., 2004), JAMIE WARD, THE STUDENT'S GUIDE TO COGNITIVE NEUROSCIENCE 4 (2d ed. 2010).

[2] DICTIONARY OF COGNITIVE SCIENCE: NEUROSCIENCE, PSYCHOLOGY, ARTIFICIAL INTELLIGENCE, LINGUISTICS, AND PHILOSOPHY xviii-xxv (Olivier Houd6 et. al. eds., Vivian Waltz trans., Psychology Press 2004) (1998).

CHAPTER FIVE

LITERATURE REVIEW

The potential contributions of neuroscience to legal decision-making are receiving more and more study in both the classroom and the courtroom. One of neuroscience's increasing functions is to provide mechanistic explanations for human behaviour and choice. To (over)simplify this nuanced terrain, it seems that there are essentially two groups in these discussions. For one, there are many who argue that free will can't exist since neuroscience has "disproven" its existence, which challenges common sense concepts of responsibility. Well-known figures in the media have declared the end of free will **(Harris, 2012; Cave, 2016)**, casting doubt on the justness of punishment as we know it **(Burns and Bechara, 2007; Sapolsky, 2017)**. Thus, the criminal justice system, which formerly relied on a now-defunct assumption of freedom and agency to impose punishment, has been fundamentally damaged and must be replaced immediately with something more enlightened and equitable.

To be sure, these ideas have sparked a lot of pushback and inspired counterarguments that try to prove the validity of conventional conceptions of legal responsibility and punitive responses to illegal behaviour. Some argue that neuroscience has no bearing on determining guilt or any common feeling of civic accountability, and that the existence of free will (if it exists at all) is irrelevant to fundamental concepts of legal obligation. This ensures that the status quo may be maintained without fear, and that the law as it now exists is not hampered by the inconsequential annoyances of predetermined acts. These counterarguments often include dismissing the importance of neuroscience in the law altogether, which may be intended as a contrecoup effect **(Morse, 2006; Pardo and Patterson, 2010; Chambon and Bigenwald, 2019)**. Obviously, these depictions are simplified caricatures of the many nuanced viewpoints included in this expanding scholarly discussion **(see, for example, Vincent Spece's work) (2013)**.

Nonetheless, many of the arguments we hear today have significant and evident common ground with either of these two extremes. We acknowledge the necessity for conservatism in developing realistic perspectives about how the legal system can alter in the wake of progress in neuroscience, without undermining the zeitgeist of this revolution or its opponents. That's why we purposefully set out to investigate the enormous territory in between the two poles of this debate. We conclude by advocating three key theses about Neurolaw and its inexorable development.

There is no shortage of scholarly and popular critiques of neuroscience's (especially neuroimaging's) place in the courtroom **(Brown and Murphy, 2010; Eagleman, 2011a; Morse, 2015; Gonzalez, 2017).** These works address the subject of the "meteoric growth" of neuroscience-based evidence in judicial decision-making, and the tone may vary from cautious to arrogant. In the courtroom, a description of neuroscience's precipitous development brings with it a rather threatening tone that may not be entirely warranted. Estimates imply that the use of neuroscience evidence in court has about doubled in the last decade **(Catley and Claydon, 2016; Farahany, 2016),** which is consistent with the field's meteoric development in the clinic and laboratory over the same time frame**(Yeung et al., 2017).** Contrary to the tone of many commentators, this continuous growth has not arrived abruptly, flooding courts with allegations that its practitioners cannot properly analyse. Over 35 years ago, in the high-profile prosecution of John Hinckley Jr. for the attempted murder of President Reagan, brain imaging was considered for the first time as evidence in a court of law **(United States vs. Hinckley, 19821).**

As the judicial system learns to incorporate and adapt to developments in clinical neuroscience, its significance in legal procedures must be carefully reviewed using established evidence standards **(Gaudet, 2011).** Still, because to the joint efforts of lawyers, scientists, and practitioners, the court is beginning to see the significance of neuroscience and neuroimaging evidence in a variety of settings. When neuroscience data might provide light on a case, courts increasingly encourage, if not insist, that it be presented as evidence **(Catley and Claydon, 2016).**

Neuroimaging may also be necessary in other situations (e.g., brain injury, degenerative disease, tumors). Of course, insanity pleas only account for a small fraction of all criminal trials, and they tend to be more successful in situations when the defendant has a history of mental health issues

(Kirschner and Galperin, 2001; Perlin, 2016). Evidentiary criteria are slightly more relaxed and lenient during sentencing arguments, when neuroscience evidence is also increasingly offered (i.e., after guilt has already been decided). This is becoming typical in instances with significant consequences, such as death punishment or life in prison, for the convicted culprit **(Miller, 2010).** When determining whether a person should get the maximum sentence or one that takes into account mitigating circumstances, such as mental health, neuroscience evidence may be deemed significant. As a matter of fact, some courts have ruled that a defence attorney who fails to bring relevant neuroscience evidence has been ineffective and has so violated a defendant's right to a fair trial **(Koenig, 2016).**

It ought to be obvious that the instruments of neuroscience are not held to lower standards than other types of evidence offered in legal arguments. In other words, its usefulness as evidence must be balanced against the risk of bias or misunderstanding among jurors. This is commonly used as a focal point by commentators, who point to the (slim) research that suggests brain imaging evidence may confuse or divert jurors from the main issues at hand **(McCabe and Castel, 2008; Weisberg et al., 2008).** Others have reviewed this evidence critically, pointing out that it was not presented in a setting similar to what jurors generally meet in trials **(Roskies et al., 2013).** In other studies that took these considerations into account, brain imaging was found to be no more credible than verbal testimony based on neuroscience **(Schweitzer and Saks, 2011; Schweitzer et al., 2011).** Furthermore, MRI-based evidence is no more convincing than other (non-neuroscience-based) evidence when subjected to cross-examination, which critically analyses the significance of material **(McCabe et al., 2011).** Lastly, the judge's function as a kind of gatekeeper for admission of evidence safeguards the system against more contentious uses of these instruments. This has been convincingly shown over and over again by the repeated rejection of fMRI by the courts as a method of lie detection, to provide just one example **(US v. Semrau, 20103 ; State v Gary Smith 20124.).** Due to the lack of adequate scientific agreement for these uses, the situation has continued. Because of this, using fMRI in this setting fails to meet the criteria of the Daubert standard for scientific evidence.

<u>AIMS AND OBJECTIVES</u>
Author's objective with the present Research Paper is to:

- Highlight and emphasize the need of improved artificial intelligence and techniques of Neuroscience as well as Cognitive Psychology in Criminal Justice system.
- Research, examine, analyze and put forth the interrelationship between Legal System, Neuroscience and Cognitive Psychology.
- Scrutinize and embellish the practical aspects of Neuroscience and Cognitive Psychology in the Criminal Legal System the way they were never involved before.
- Give a more contributory approach through this paper to the legal system for its modernization, revolution and evolution with time.

RESEARCH QUESTIONS

Author in this Research Paper wants to deal with following questions and challenges as faced by the Indian Legal System while considering neuroscience and cognitive psychology as an acceptable revolutionizing techniques for Indian Legal System:-

- Whether neuroscience and cognitive psychology can prove to be a boon in reforming the fundamental concepts of Indian Legal System?
- Whether it is ethically and morally appropriate within the circumference of concepts ofCriminology to use a scientific approach towards offenders?
- Whether the said approach has the accuracy to be placed a reliance upon in evidentiary aspects by Indian Judiciary?
- Whetherthis technique reliable in studying the convicts mind of whether he will resort to reoffending?

HYPOTHESIS

Ha- Improved artificial intelligence and techniques of Neuroscience as well as Cognitive Psychology can revolutionize the Criminal Justice system.

Ha- Modern Courts are the aspects to be adopted from Courts in U.S.A. to be adopted in the field of Neuroscience and Cognitive Psychology in the Criminal Legal System the way they were never involved before.

RESEARCH MENTHOLOGY

Doctrinal Research Method has been adopted followed by qualitative approach and applied research strategy wherein the author has used both primary and secondary sources of data collection from various legislative write-ups, case laws, online sources, articles, research papers etc. .

• <u>Neuroscience and Cognitive Psychology in Police Investigation</u>

Two elements have been highlighted so far by the author as constituting criminal liability. in comparison to Actus Reus and Mens Rea wherein, for instance, a defendant is only guilty of Larceny if he (a) took something (b) that belonged to someone else (c) without permission, I while (ii) knowing that he was taking it, (iii) knowing that there was a substantial risk that it belonged to someone else, (iv) intending never to return it. In general terms, the 'actusreus' of a crime refers to the external circumstances that must be shown in order to prove that a defendant satisfies a legislative definition of a crime, such as (a), (b), and (c).

The mental state of the perpetrator, including I (ii), (iii), and (iv), is the'mensrea' of the crime. However, several components typically categorised as actusreus contain information about the defendant's mind, therefore these are simply approximate definitions of 'actusreus' and'mensrea. Proof that a person's mind was directing his body's motions is necessary to establish that he was, for example, involved in the act of taking anything; a person who is carrying a loaf of bread when someone tosses him out the door of the bakery has not "taken" the loaf. Knowledge about the person's mental state is insufficient, though. Further, it's important to establish that he was in possession of the item and removed it from the reach of its rightful owner. The actus-reus of a crime consists of the external circumstances necessary for conviction rather than the mental states of the accused. In contrast, elements I (ii), (iii), and (iv) all have to do with the criminal's state of mind, or mensrea.Even law recognizes variety of mental states as the science does. Police officials in their daily routine investigations seek various types of information to conclude to the offenders and catch them red handed in time-bound manner. For technical glitches and skills they tend to seek help of crime branch and court transfers the case to same. Due to lack of technological developments in this field in India, forensics also lags its helping hand to the Police Officials.

CHAPTER SIX

NEUROSCIENCE AND COGNITIVE PSYCHLOGY IN COURT ROOMS

MICHAEL CASE[1]

Michael, who had no prior history of criminal behaviour, acquired a sudden interest in child pornography at the age of 40. If he agrees to go through a treatment programme for sexually molesting a kid, he may escape going to prison for the crime he committed against a 12-year-old girl. Michael was able to get away more easily, and an MRI later showed that he had a tumour in the orbitofrontal cortex. After having his tumour removed, he no longer felt any of those compulsions. It seemed like the tumour had returned, but it was surgically removed this time. The finest example of criminal anomalies might be found in this instance.

PEOPLE V. NEWTON[2]

The defendant shot the officer because he had been injured in the stomach by accident during the mob lynching. Therefore, he was exonerated since his post-traumatic consequences from the injuries were a contributing factor in his criminal behaviour.

PEOPLE V. WEINSTEIN[3]

After Weinstein was arrested and charged with second-degree murder for allegedly killing his one and only wife by strangling her and then hurling her from the 12th floor, his legal team began to suspect that his conduct was abnormal. The PET scan revealed that he had an arachnoid cyst. As a result, he was eventually given the opportunity to enter a guilty plea to manslaughter.

DAUBERT V. MERRELL DOW PHARMACEUTICALS, INC.[4]

In one instance, the corporation was sued by a grieving family after they were accused of profiting from the deaths of two unborn children. As a result of this case and the defendant company's persistent refusal to appear in court, the US Supreme Court replaced the Fyre Standard of Admissibility with the Daubert Standard of admissibility, making it possible for scientific instruments and methods to be presented as evidence in lower courts.

R. V. HENDY[5]

Murder charges were brought against Hendy. Hendy was a heavy drinker who once assaulted a buddy at a party. The murder was attributed to him since everyone thought he did it in a fit of wrath. Nonetheless, further examination revealed that Hendy had consumed food and a non-alcoholic beverage that day. Subsequently, he stabbed a total stranger 18 times to death, wrote an apologetic message to his mom, and dumped his body along his road. When it happened, he was just 16 years old. The following decision was reached by the court based on the expert's testimony: "the Applicant had sustained a brain injury during a vehicle collision." The Applicant may have suffered damage to his temporal lobe, the region of the brain responsible for self-control and learning, as a result of the accident, he says. A major motif, in his opinion, was the Applicant's depression and growing awareness that he was flawed. The physician concluded that he was not thinking like a typical juvenile offender. He concluded that "it was quite likely that the Applicant had experienced a mild to moderate degree of brain pathology at some time, notably in the left temporal lobe, but that his difficulties were more complicated than being simply attributable to this."Subsequent to conviction of Hendy, EEG techniques were adopted in use for reaching at conclusive evidence.

R V. HALLING[6]

In this case, only expert judgement and scientific evidence could decide whether Hallingshould be held criminally accountable for murder or not. A case that lacks neuroscientific evidence will not be rejected if other evidence is adequate, but will be dismissed if no other evidence is sufficient.

R V. HOLDSWORTH[7]

In a case involving the likely cause of a child's death, neurologists provided thorough expert testimony before the appeals court. Holdsworth, the nanny, was found guilty of the girl's murder. The new expert testimony caused her conviction to be overturned, and a new trial was mandated. Due to the complexity of the evidence, the appeals court suggested using case management, saying, "we give permission to appeal and overturn the

Applicant's murder conviction." We note in closing that intensive case management will be necessary for any retrial. To that end, we call your attention to the comments made by this court in R v. Harris [2005] EWCA Crim 1980.... on the court's ability to arrange for experts to confer and, ideally, reach consensus on areas of agreement and disagreement and a statement of their rationales.

R V. HARRIS, R. V. ROCK, R. V. CHERRY, R V. FLAUDER[8]

The aforementioned Sudden Infant Death (SID) lawsuits rest on the premise that determining the cause of death via neuropathology relies too much on scientific and medical reasoning. In addition, it was determined that the neuropathology of death has been employed as a final approach to resolve the issue in a number of appeals, which highlights the need for improved developmental and neuro-scientific methods.

R. V. CANNINGS[9]

The appeals court in this instance took into account neuroscientific findings and spoke with 10 experts. The main point of contention was whether or not, in light of recent scientific discoveries, the standard method of diagnosis for illegal attacks on minors is valid. All of the babies were diagnosed with NAHI (Non Accidental Head Injury). The investigation concluded that the shaking had produced the triad of injuries. In court, Dr. Jennein Geddes presented a competing theory. The court carefully considered the diagnosis and the testimony of all experts before reaching the following detailed decision about the defendant's mental capacity: It is required to outline some of the anatomy involved in words which may be understood by laymen and which, from a medical perspective, may appear relatively basic in order to illustrate the two ideas. First, to aid the reader, we have included a medical terminology glossary (appendix A) and schematics of the human brain (appendix B) (appendix B). There are three encasing membranes for the brain. The pia mater is the membrane that covers the brain. Spiders are up next. The subarachnoid space is the region between the pia and arachnoid. The dura is the third membrane, beginning at the base of the brain and continuing down to protect the spinal cord. The subdural space is the area between the dura and the arachnoid. Veins that connect the dura to the arachnoid are referred to as "bridging veins."

The falx, which is a component of the dura, separates the two sides of the brain, also known as the cerebral hemispheres. The craniocervical junction, as its name suggests, is the point in the neck where the brain and spinal cord are united below the cerebral hemispheres. From the brain, the spinal cord travels via the foramen magnum and into the spine.

The court concluded with the following statement: "Much effort by committed men and women is devoted to this subject. One pressing goal should be to eliminate, or at least drastically decrease, the number of child deaths and parent losses that occur each year. But in the process, we may learn a lot about fatalities that aren't accidents and are instead the direct result of bad parenting. We can't help but wonder whether, in light of the ongoing medical research being conducted here and across the world, some of the honest opinions voiced with reasonable confidence in the current case (on both sides of the dispute) may have to be amended in the years to come. There is no guarantee that tomorrow's explanations will be any clearer than today's. A counter-challenge should be issued to any dogmatic claims till then.

<u>SHARIF'S CASE[10]</u>

Sharif was found guilty of conspiracy to defraud, but his conviction was contested on the grounds that he suffered from mental impairment at the time of the alleged crime. To ensure that no miscarriage of justice occurs, the Court of Appeal established the Criminal Cases Review Commission (CCRC) to conduct investigations into pending appeals. Sharif's father made the argument that his son's recent head injury, the consequence of a robbery at the family business, was causing him emotional and physical distress. In spite of mounting evidence, Sharif maintained his denial of any involvement in the fraud operation. After reviewing the footage, it became abundantly evident that Sharif seemed absolutely unremarkable throughout the committing of the crime. The prosecution said, "Her judgement was that, if indeed the appellant was represented on the films and who had carried out the execution of some other papers as stated by the prosecution, he was not suffering from any major mental disease and should be deemed as competent to plead." She didn't give much credence to the idea that he had a diagnosable mental or biological brain problem.

Instead of responding to the question of whether he pleads guilty or not, Sharif remained silent. As a result, the Court of Appeals mandated more expert testimony. In light of the fact that Sharif is being detained as'mute of malice,' a not guilty plea was contemplated on his behalf. The court ordered an MRI after discovering Sharif had an enlarged brain. Moderate widespread atrophy of the brain was seen. However, a medical evaluation revealed that Sharif was competent to stand trial. At first, there were two separate reports. The first report included data from an MRI performed in January 2000, which "showed that the appellant's neurological state had worsened since trial." The opinions of Greater Manchester Neuroscience Centre Professor Neary were included in a second report prepared in March 2001. He speculated that the appellant's condition was chronic and degenerative in nature, with ties to his parents' consanguinity and an autosomal ailment. According to neuropsychiatric geneticist Dr. David Crauford, "the clinical picture is strongly suggestive of a severe degenerative disorder of the central nervous system," and "the most likely explanation for the appellant's medical problems is a previously unrecognised autosomal recessive disorder occurring as a result of multiple consanguineous marriages in his family." The CCRC consulted with other specialists and arrived at the conclusion that Sharif's father was the true mastermind behind the whole operation. The court's indulgence of so many different perspectives and neuroscientific methods in this case was really remarkable. Sharif's conviction was overturned as a result.

BROWN V. ENTERTAINMENT MERCHANT'S ASSOCIATION[11]

The 2005 California legislation prohibiting the sale of some violent video games to minors without parental supervision was overturned by the US Supreme Court in a historic ruling. The Supreme Court voted 7-2 to strike down the legislation and uphold earlier court rulings, finding that video games are entitled to the same First Amendment protections as other types of communication. The verdict was seen as a major triumph for the video gaming sector. Given the dynamic nature of video games and their rapidly developing technology, some justices on the Court hinted that the matter would need to be revisited in the future.

MADISON V. ALABAMA[12]

Madison is accused of murdering Police Officer Julius Schulte in April 1985 in Mobile, Alabama. Schulte was shot twice in the back of the head. During a domestic dispute between Madison and his ex-girlfriend, Schulte stepped in to mediate; Madison ended up shooting and wounding his ex. Madison has been incarcerated at Holman Correctional Facility ever since September of 1985. It was in the context of this amendment that the Supreme Court heard the case known as Madison v. Alabama. The issue at hand is whether the Eighth Amendment forbids executing a person for a crime they do not recall committing.

ELMORE V. HOLBROOK[13]

Claimant Clark Elmore was found guilty of first-degree murder in 1995 and given a death sentence. His court-appointed attorney was familiar with

Elmore's history of impulsive conduct and exposure to poisons as a young adult, but had never handled a capital case before. Elmore's lawyer was advised by a more seasoned attorney to look into the possibility that Elmore had brain injury when he was younger. Instead of doing so, or even performing a little research into Elmore's background, Elmore's attorney spent an hour arguing to the jury that Elmore felt remorse for his crime during the punishment phase of the trial. The fact that Elmore had spent his youth playing in fields poisoned with pesticides and his military duty repairing Agent Orange pumps was thus not presented to the jury. The jury was denied access to the evidence of specialists who testified that Elmore suffered from cognitive impairment and lacked the ability to regulate his impulses. In spite of several independent witnesses attesting to Elmore's profound regret, the jury only heard from a collection of local judges that he looked "dejected" when he pled guilty to murder.

KAHLER V. KANSAS[14]

Since at least the time of English common law, the insanity defence has been a popular affirmative defence. The M'Naghten principles, which have been cited in some form in both American and British law, imply that a person may be held not guilty of a crime if they suffer from a mental illness that prevents them from either directing their acts or understanding whether their conduct were right or wrong. is a case in which the Supreme Court of the United States held that the insanity defence should not be used in criminal proceedings when the defendant's capacity to distinguish right from wrong was at issue. A decision was issued on March 23, 2020, after the case was heard on October 7, 2019.

SEARS V. UPTON [15]

Counsel's failure to introduce evidence of defendant's experiences in the Korean War — he was in two battles that resulted in the death of countless soldiers around him and left him with extreme emotional scars — was held to be ineffective assistance of counsel that would have changed the outcome of the trial, reversing the Eleventh Circuit's decision. All nine justices agreed that any jury could not have failed to be moved by his courageous service throughout these terrible wars. The state's trial counsel was deficient since they did not look into any mitigating evidence that would have prevented the death sentence. The state court's approach for deciding whether prejudice existed was improper, thus the Supreme Court remanded for a fresh assessment of prejudice that takes into account all of the material produced in the post-conviction proceedings.

J.D.B. V. NORTH CAROLINA [16]

In this decision, the Supreme Court of the United States reversed its own rule from seven years earlier and declared that age and mental condition are significant for assessing police custody for Miranda reasons. J.D.B., a special education student aged 13, was a suspect in two robberies, according to the police. J.D.B. was questioned by a police investigator, a uniformed police officer, and school administrators during a visit to his school. J.D.B. ultimately admitted guilt and was sentenced to prison. Neither the Miranda warning nor a chance for J.D.B.'s legal guardian to be present during the interview were provided.

TAPIA V. UNITED STATES[17]

Alejandra Tapia received a 51-month jail term for smuggling an undocumented worker into the United States. Tapia contested the District Court's rationale for imposing his sentence. For his part, Tapia argued that his sentence shouldn't be determined by when he could be eligible for the Bureau of Prisons' substance abuse treatment programme. The Ninth Circuit Court of Appeals upheld the lower court's ruling in a short order, citing precedent. was a case decided by the Supreme Court of the United States in which it was decided that a federal court may not extend a defendant's sentence in order to help them change their ways and become productive members of society.

SCHIRIRO V. LANDRIGON[18]

The Supreme Court of the United States upheld the lower court's authority to rule that defendant could not establish a factual record, even with the benefit of an evidentiary hearing, that would entitle him to habeas relief. As the record showed that defendant would have interrupted and refused to allow his counsel to disclose any such information, the Court found that defendant could not claim prejudice from any failure of counsel to seek more mitigating evidence. The record also revealed that defendant was aware of what would happen if mitigation evidence wasn't allowed, and that the facts defendant wanted to establish in an evidentiary hearing were, at most, poor mitigation evidence that wouldn't have impacted the outcome. Therefore, the Appellate Court's decision was overturned, and the matter was sent back to the lower court for additional consideration.

PORTER V. MCCOLLUM[19]

The United States Supreme Court ruled that Porter's attorney's performance was inadequate, and the Florida Supreme Court interpreted Strickland in an illogical manner to conclude that Porter was not disadvantaged by the ineffective representation. The Supreme Court ruled that the attorney's failure to do even a little research into Porter's past demonstrates that his performance was not up to a reasonable standard. The Court also found that the state court's finding that the sentence would not have been different had the judge and jury heard the substantial mitigating evidence Porter's attorney did not locate or submit was objectively unreasonable.

BEARD V. BANKS[20]

When it was shown that the restriction was essential to urge improved conduct from exceptionally tough convicts who had previously been deprived of practically all privileges, the Supreme Court of the United States concluded that there was adequate basis for the regulation. Prisoner submitted a cross-motion for summary judgement arguing that the rule was irrational as a matter of law, but provided no evidence to rebut Secretary's summary judgement evidence.

DURHAM V. UNITED STATES[21]

An accused is not legally accountable if his illegal behaviour was the consequence of mental sickness or mental defect, as stated in this criminal case that later became known as the Durham rule for jurors to determine a person is not guilty by reason of insanity. The purpose of this was to allow psychiatrists to "inform the jury about the nature of [the defendant's mental disorder]" so that jurors may be "directed by greater vistas of information concerning mental life" while making decisions. The case served as inspiration. Only two states at the time accepted it, but it continues to have an impact on discussions over what constitutes legal insanity. The ruling was criticised for not defining mental illness, for leaving the jury reliant on expert evidence, and for not providing a criteria by which to determine impairment of reason or control.

KYLLO V. UNITED STATES [22]

The employment of a FLIR thermal imaging system from a public vantage point to monitor the heat radiated from a person's house was deemed to be a "search" within the meaning of the Fourth Amendment in a 5–4 ruling that cut across ideological lines.

[1][1]Jeffrey M. Burns & Russell H. Swerdlow, *Right Orbitofrontal Tumor With Pedophilia Symptom and Constructional Apraxia Sign*, 60 arch. neurol. 437, 440 (2003).

[2]People v. Newton (8 Cal. App. 3d 359 (Ct. App. 1970))

[3] The People of State of Illinois v. Weinstein 35 Ill. 2d 467 (1966) 220 N.E.2d 432

[4]DAUBERT V. MERRELL DOW PHARMACEUTICALS, INC. 509 U.S. 579 (1993)

[5](2006) EWCA 819.

[6] (Jason) [2021] EWCA Crim. 1774.

[7][2008] EWCA Crim 971

[8][2005] EWCA Crim 1980.

[9]*R v Cannings* [2004] EWCA Crim 1

[10]R v. Mohd.Sharif [2010] EWCA Crim 1709.

[11]564 U.S. 786 (2011).

[12], 586 U.S. (2019).

[13]580 U.S. (2016).

[14] 589 U.S. (2020)

[15] 130 S. Ct. 3259 (2010)

[16] 564 U.S. 261 (2011),

[17] 564 U.S. 319 (2011),

[18]550 U.S. 465 (2007).

[19]558 U.S. (2009).

[20]548 U.S. 521 (more) 126 S. Ct. 2572; 165 L. Ed. 2d 697

[21] 214 F.2d 862 (D.C. Cir. 1954),

[22] 533 U.S. 27 (2001),

CHAPTER SEVEN

GROWTH OF NEUROSCIENCE AND COGNIOTIVE PSYCHOLOGY IN INDIA

The National Institute of Mental Health and Neurosciences (NIMHANS) was founded in 1970, marking a significant turning point in the birth and development of neuroscience in India. Central Drug Research Institute, Lucknow had an International Research Paper session on "**Central Synaptic Transmission**" the same year. As this chapter will explain in further detail, the first major institution dedicated to neuroscience did not appear until many years later, in the form of the Indian Academy of Neurosciences. Some of the most notable national research institutes in the fields of Neuroscience and Cognitive Psychology are:-

- National Center For Biological Sciences (NCBS)
- Institute For Stem Cell Biology and Regenerative Medicine (Instem)
- National Brain Research Center (NBRS)
- Centre of Behavior and Cognitive Sciences (CBCS).

The worldwide top nations in said field are U.S.A., China, United Kingdom, Germany, Canada, Italy, Japan, Australia, France, Netherlands, Spain and Brazil.In the past five years, India has been ranked 15th in terms of citable documents in neurosciences with U.S.A at top position.

CHAPTER EIGHT

COGNITIVE SCIENCE RESEARCH INITIATIVE

- **Introduction**

The Cognitive Science Research Initiative (CSRI) was established by the United States Department of Science and Technology to investigate the human mind, brain, and the ways in which these organs influence one's mental state and one's ability to manipulate one's environment. Those plans were implemented in 2008 as part of India's 11th Year Plan. To better comprehend Indian thought, it advocates for more funding for interdisciplinary studies of cognitive science.

- **Objectives**

- The mission of the Cognitive Science Research Initiative is to transform a wide range of disciplines, including those studying the biological, social, and pharmacological roots of mental illness.
- Creation of more effective instructional materials and pedagogical models.
- Design of superior software technologies and artificial intelligence gadgets.
- Eliminating duplication in developing and analysing social policies.

CHAPTER NINE

INDIAN ACADEMY OF NEUROSCIENCES

In 1982, a group of highly regarded researchers in India established the Indian Academy of Neurosciences (IAN). The Academy's mission since its foundation has been to advance the field of neurosciences.

Through the election of Fellows and Honorary Fellows, the Academy honours outstanding members of the Neuroscience community. To honour scientists who have made significant contributions to the field of neuroscience, the Academy created the BK Bachhawat Life Time Achievement Award and the KT Shetty Memorial Oration. The Academy has established prizes for both oral and written presentations in order to motivate budding scientists. To help defray the costs of attending the Indian Academy of Neurosciences' annual meeting, the Academy offers awards Travel Fellowships to deserving individuals.

There is a healthy mix of both fundamental and clinical scientists in the Indian Academy of Neurosciences. Though it began with a modest number of neuroscientists in 1982, the Academy has now grown to include more than 900 life members from countries as diverse as India, Germany, Japan, Poland, Saudi Arabia, Sri Lanka, South Africa, the United Kingdom, and the United States.

NATIONAL INSTITUTE OF MENTAL HEALTH AND NEURO SCIENCES (NIMHANS)

Karnataka's National Institute of Mental Health and Neurosciences (NIMHANS) has been around since the 1940s, when it was founded as part of the British colonial administration. Many advances in the treatment of mental illness were made in the medical care of the region when it was under British and colonial authority. In the 1980s, the British government funded the creation of a mental institution and institute known as AIIMH, which subsequently merged to become NIHMANS.

NATIONAL CENTER FOR BIOLOGICAL SCIENCES (NCBS)

The National Center for Biomedical Sciences (NCBS) is a world-class research facility outfitted with everything a scientist could possibly need to further his or her knowledge, conduct experiments, and conduct other types of research. They focus on cutting-edge research in the biological sciences. The Tata Institute for Fundamental Research includes this institution. The study of individual molecules, cells, and organisms is complemented by computer modelling. This prestigious national lab's overarching mission is to develop a holistic understanding of life's processes by exploring biology at all levels.

NATIONAL BRAIN RESEARCH CENTRE (NBRS)

The National Brain Research Centre is India's preeminent centre for neuroscience study and training. The interdisciplinary methods used by NBRC's scientists and students span the fields of biology, computer science, mathematics, physics, engineering, medicine, and more. NBRC is a Deemed-to-be University and autonomous institution situated in the Aravali foothills in Manesar, Haryana. It receives funding from the Department of Biotechnology, Government of India. The Government of India has designated NBRC as an Institution of Excellence.

CENTRE OF BEHAVOURIAL AND COGNITIVE SCIENCES (CBCS)

The Centre for Brain and Cognitive Sciences (CBCS) was formally inaugurated on February 2, 2003, by the then Minister of Human Resource Development of the Government of India. The Centre offers doctoral and master'sprogrammes in the field of neuroscience and cognitive sciences to help students advance their knowledge and expertise in these areas. It is also well-known for its pioneering outreach initiatives and cutting-edge research across a wide range of fields within the behavioural and cognitive sciences. CBCS is a centre that promotes research into emerging interdisciplinary connections and works to strengthen established ones, with a particular emphasis on the fields of computer science, neuroscience, psychology, linguistics, philosophy, and the social sciences. In the field of behavioural and cognitive sciences, the University of Allahabad has been recognised as a "ISLAND OF EXCELLENCE" thanks to the "University Grants Commission Scheme" for universities with the potential to excel. The Centre houses seven laboratories (the Cognitive Neuroscience Lab, the Neuroinformatics and Intelligent Computing Lab, the Visual Cognition Lab, the Language Cognition Lab, the Bio-feedback Lab, the Virtual Reality

Lab, and the Neuropsychology and Rehabilitation Lab) where researchers and students can conduct experiments and learn new techniques in various branches of cognitive science.

INSTITUTE FOR STEM CELL SCIENCE AND REGENERATIVE MEDICINE (inSTEM)

When it comes to stem cell science and regenerative medicine, InStem is in the vanguard of research institutions. inStem's work investigates fundamental questions in regenerative biology through the use of model organisms, the development of platforms to interrogate signalling pathways with novel chemical entities, the modelling of human diseases using stem cells, the examination of clinical manifestations of diseases that can potentially be treated by stem cells, and the development of tools. Research is conducted in teams that have common interests and work together to create novel approaches to problems that go beyond the scope of any one lab. Highlighted The aforementioned institution's publications have provided enough resourcefulness to enlightenment of numerous learners in the subject in question.

- ## Does Free will matters in Criminal Responsibility

Criminal Responsibility is nothing but the ingredients present behind a criminal offence vis-à-vis Mens Rea and Actus Rea. Foundations of responsibility are avoiding wrongdoing or acting otherwise. [1]The notion of determinism, as put forward by neuroscience, by reducing each of our actions to their neurological and unconscious causes, and therefore treating them as mere events rather than wilful actions, would appear to render the possibility of alternative outcomes illusory. Consequently, we would not be responsible, unless some other notion could be identified to salvage human agency and thus, responsibility itself. Criminal responsibility is not founded in free will but on practical, subjective and political considerations.[2] Some legal and popular expressions may lead us to think that responsibility is nonetheless grounded in free will. Everyone legitimately assumes, for example, that criminal proceedings aim at evaluating if the accused "could have acted otherwise." H.L.A. Hart, famous legal philosopher, takes the "fair chance of avoiding wrongdoing" to be the foundation of criminal responsibility.

Making a choice versus Having a choice

The indiscriminate use of the word "choice" in popular psychology is something that Shepard and O'Grady are critical of. A recent empirical study demonstrates that the expressions "making a choice" and "having a choice" refer to two separate although connected ideas of choice. The authors state that there is a distinction between the two ideas because of the different types of options that each one takes into account. The presence or absence of actually open alternatives has little effect on the decision-making process, but the presence or absence of psychologically open alternatives and the agent's decision-making process do matter much. Instead, the freedom to make a decision depends on whether or not there are realistic and acceptable alternatives. Both Shepard and O'Grady link this divergence in thinking to an evaluation of free will (which in turn they relate to responsibility). They observe that "findings show attributions of free will more closely reflect attributions of making a choice than having a choice," despite the fact that few research have studied this relationship between choice and free will, with inconsistent results. [3]

The Morse Challenge

Morse Challenge is a theory propounded by S.J. Morse at the verges where both Law and Neuroscience meet. His idea goes as follows:

Nothing "just as it is" necessitates "what ought to be," without the supposition that "what ought to be" (what is desirable) should be in line with "what is." Brain imaging cannot be relied upon to establish the line between normal and pathological in ethics or the law, as he argues in his seminal work "Brain overclaim syndrome and responsibility: a diagnostic comment." We can rule out the possibility of blame being placed on the brain. People who play roles in drama include"

In his famous article "Brain overclaim syndrome[4] and responsibility: a diagnostic note" he recalls the behavioral, as opposed to cerebral, criteria for responsibility and insists on the incapacity of brain imaging to set the threshold of normality vs. abnormality either in ethics or in law. "Brains are not responsible. Acting people are" [5] It has been held in one of the judgements that lack of responsibility is something irrelevant to the concept of death penalty for an offence.[6] According to **Barteschi,** responsibility is nothing but a normative concept believed in accordance with the principles and rules set based on personal theories deviating from reality just like the concept of God.

LIMITATIONS OF NEUROSCIENCE AND COGNITIVE PSYCHOLOGY
Legal Limitations

Neuroscience and cognitive psychology can have their impact rendered merely on **legal excuses** and not on **legal justifications**. Arguments relating to neurological conditions reducing possible options (such as "my brain was in such a state that it was impossible to avoid acting a particular way" or "my brain did it, not I") do not intervene at this stage. Justifications do not only tackle phenomena out of will power's reach (like electrical pulses in neural circuits), but precisely phenomena completely independent and external to the agent, including its neural circuits. Justifications are about circumstances external to oneself, or even actually contrary to oneself since all the goodwill in the world could not prevent wrongdoing. This is the case with self-defense, for example, when circumstances someone faces only allow for two options - kill or be killed-, knowing that the latter option constitutes the threshold beyond which obedience becomes illegitimate. Necessity" is another legal justification that follows the same rationale, although more flexible as it allows the possibility of choosing between two evils. Aristotle notoriously illustrated the situation of a mixed act (intentional but constrained) through the story of a captain's ship.[7]

Any evidence or representation made before the court undergoes the **test of admissibility.** Standards for the same have been made out in **Fyre's Test.**[8]Similarly certain limitations were levied on genetic evidences and their admissibility.[9] The Daubert Test establishes the following admissibility conditions: (1) the expert report must be based on sufficient facts and data; (2) the testimony is based on reliable principles and methods; and (3) those principles and methods have been faithfully applied to the facts in question. Those criteria are, however, neither exhaustive nor exclusive, and others have been developed: whether the evidence submitted belongs to the expert's usual field of research or on the contrary have been elaborated in anticipation of the trial.[10]There is a need to make constructive alternative considerations[11] and interpretations during a trial for which expert advise is sought for various technical implications to be reached to in a matter.[12]A clear approach towards setting up standards of admissibility was made pertaining to both general standards and standards pertaining to various scientific tools in **Harrington v. State** recently[13]

LIE DETECTORS

A P-300 MERMER test with its universally accepted full form as **Memory and Encoding Related Multifaceted Electroencephalographic Responseor Dr. Farwell's brain fingerprinting** is not exactly a lie detector.

Rather, it highlights the accused's memory, or absence thereof, about certain facts, by measuring a positive brain wave called P300 MERMER. A certain wave potential obtained through relevant stimulus would show the presence of an actual memory linked to this stimulus. Proponents of this technique measure the wave amplitude from P300 responses to images or words linked to familiar events or events recognized by the accused: a crime, terrorist training, bomb-crafting knowledge, etc. The test produces a neural signature for the absence or presence of relevant information in the accused's memory, and gives a reliability index for that result. Experiments in and outside the laboratory have shown an error ratio of less than 1% .P-300 MERMER test has been used in a somewhat contradictory manner in the courts: in <u>Harrington v. State (2003)</u> (**Supra**) it allowed for the release of a man wrongly convicted of murder after 23 years of imprisonment. However, in **State v. Grinder[14]**, it has been recognized as a highly probative and incriminating evidence

Technical Limitations

<u>TEMPORAL LIMITATIONS</u>

Techniques and tools of neuroscience such as MRI, Brain imaging etc. are fruitful in identification of and proving permanent abnormalities pertaining to mind but, temporary conditions concurrent to time, situation, circumstances and events cannot be anticipated.

<u>INTERPRETATIVE LIMITATIONS</u>

A first limit relates to the interpretation of functional imaging data (e.g., fMRI) and the risk of evidential circularity. It remains difficult to accurately map a cognitive process or function in a precise brain area, neural network or population. This difficulty arises from the fact that one brain area can perform different functions (many-to-one mapping) that are hardly distinguishable without an appropriate experimental protocol. Partially overlapping activity patterns associated with distinctive functions also complicates the proper interpretation of brain scans when they are not concurrently read with the patient's behavior (for example, when neural circuits required for an action's execution partially overlap with some linked to the observation of that same action executed by a third party, if not with the simple imagination of that action. Hence, exclusive neural evidence, just as strictly behavioral evidence, does not solve Wootton's circularity issue mentioned above. Furthermore, looking at the circumstances surrounding the alleged crime is necessary. Because brain scans are rarely informative in themselves – without referring to the behavior they seek to explain – there are few situations in which they are useful for establishing criminal liability. They may only be in distinguishing the truth in "gray area" cases "in which the behavioral evidence is unclear"

A second linked limit is the risk of producing reverse inferences i.e., inferring a mental process from the observation of activity patterns without consideration for the actual behavior or the circumstances thereof. Reverse inferences can lead to fallacious interpretations of neuroimaging data such as: concluding that a blind woman sees because her visual cortex activates; or coming to the conclusion that dogs understand words of praise because some patterns, as revealed by fMRI, activate in their left brain hemisphere. It is worth noting that reverse inferences are often wrongly used as a common strategy to interpret experiment results. The problem is that neuroscience still does not have a sufficient understanding of brain functions to infer mental process on the sole basis of neural activity. Reverse inferences, although tolerated in the context of exploratory scientific practices, is thus not fit for law's requirements, in particular considering the institution of criminal responsibility and the major consequences it brings about for an incriminated individual.[15]

COMPARATIVE LIMITATIONS

For an effective and conclusive results with accuracy, results obtained from tools and techniques of neuroscience and cognitive need to undergo group analysis. However, what is measured is an indirect effect of brain activity, i.e., a modification of oxygen levels in local blood supplies (blood-oxygen-level-dependent response, or BOLD signal). This measurement is considered as a reliable indicium of a specific brain area being required to do a task, if not essentially "doing" that task. However, linking BOLD signal variations to cognitive processes remains difficult for three reasons: (1) even in a resting state, the brain presents spontaneous activity fluctuations; (2) neural computations have intrinsic noise; (3) what one does or what one thinks in a scan can never be completely controlled. It is thus imperative, before introducing fMRI scans in courtrooms, to conceive experiments carefully designed to isolate, in an individual's brain, activity fluctuations relevant to the behavior being studied, i.e., experiments (factorial or parametric designs) that discriminate between relevant neural activity and background or task-unrelated neural activity.

NORMATIVE LIMITATIONS

The relevance of results, be they from functional or anatomical scans, depends on the (normative) definition of handicap linked to a certain behavior. For example, anatomical scans (the equivalent of pictures of the brain structure) can reveal anatomical alterations and anomalies (e.g., loss of cerebral matter, alteration in the organic structure, excessive spinal fluid, etc.). Relevantly producing such evidence, however, implies the hypothesis that those anomalies alter the accused's capacity to follow or detect a norm, or to adapt to or adopt an appropriate behavior. Anatomical anomalies alone do not indicate the presence of a handicap, and do not necessarily translate into mental deficiencies.[16]

- EXPERIMENTAL LIMITATIONS

Due to unavailability of accessibility towards equipments, resources, vast infrastructure, technological developments, grant for experimentation, conducts of experimentation and laboratories, it becomes highly inconvenient as well as explicitly hard to device mechanisms for accurate results through brain tools.

RESULT, DISCUSSION AND CONCLUSION

The interaction of neuroscience and law, i.eNeurolawis considered to offer fairness to the law in a practical sense and can help the legal instrument that regulates the human behaviour to hold justice to make it more reasonable.

In India we need a system efficient enough for speedy disposal of matters along with recognition of the criminals behind an offence with a view of increasing crime rate so that people can have their trust back on the Judicial System as well as the investigation system.

Apart from the need of technological advancements, resources and neuroscientists, we need to have amendments in the prevailing law of evidence act as well as we need a completely new legislation for going far ahead in the matters of justice.

The Neurolaw shall help lawyers to show before the judge the functioning of the brain and its associated behaviouralcorrelates which is relevant to the case at hand. It shall also help lawyers to produce neuro-scientific data to assist an expert in offering his opinion most scientifically to make justice fairer.

Neurolaw, shall help, for the proof of a liability, to expand the scope of law, enhancing the knowledge of a judge in respect to a legal right, to gain mature understanding of normative phenomena in terms of brain, mind, psychological insights to revisit various legal concepts and various rules of liabilities and rights. It shall also help expand the frontier of jurisprudence.

[1]Note that the definition of free will is contentious in itself. According to Frankfurt, an agent is "free" if he wants what he wants, such that his lower-order desires correspond to higher-order volitions (e.g., Frankfurt, 1988). For others (Descartes, Berkeley, Kant), free will requires that an agent can genuinely escape the causal necessity of a deterministic world.

[2]   https://www.frontiersin.org/articles/10.3389/fpsyg.2019.01406/full#note5

[3]Shepard and Reuter, 2012; Nahmias and Thompson, 2014; Nahmias et al., 2014.

[4]S.J. Morse, with humor, considers such arguments as *the signs of a disorder that I have preliminarily entitled Brain Overclaim Syndrome*" (Morse, 2006, p. 397).

[5]This echoes a recent argument from Krakauer et al. (2017) in favor of *behaviourally* driven neuroscience: neuroscience needs behavior to make sense of neural findings. As a matter of fact, the *neural* implementation of behavior is always better investigated after having first carefully studied (i.e., theoretically and experimentally decomposed) the behavior itself (Krakauer et al., 2017; see also infra, "Technical limitations").

[6]Rooper v. Simmons 543 U.S. 551 (2005).

[7]^ The act is intentional, but constrained. This type of excuse acknowledges the presence of *mensrea*: in *the Nicomachean Ethics*, Aristotle illustrates the situation of a mixed act by using the image of a captain's ship in a storm who must abandon his shipment to save his crew. In this case, the captain's action results from the captain's choice, and hence it is still a voluntary action even though the action was constrained by external causes.

^ For example, the notion of self-defense is sometimes used to illustrate a claim about responsibility, including in cautious and relevant articles (e.g., Haggard, 2017).

[8]Fyre v. United States 293 F. 1013.

[9] Cullen v. Pinholster 563 U.S. 170 (2011)

[10]Daubert v. Merrel Dow Pharmaceuticals Inc. 509 U.S. 579 (1993).

[11]Claar v. Burlington 106 F.3d 411.

[12]Kumho Tire Company v. Carmichael 526 U.S. 137 (1999); General Electric Company v. Joiner 522 U.S. 136 (1997).

[13]395 U.S. 250 (1969).

1. [15] A number of articles have interpreted this result as signifying that dogs *understand* human words because lexical processing is associated with a similar pattern of activation in the left hemisphere in most humans (but see also Andics et al., 2017, *Erratum for the Report "Neural mechanisms for lexical processing in dogs"*).

2. ^ Among other examples, there are inconsistencies in brain areas associated with moral reasoning: utilitarian decisions (sacrificing one life to save three others) in the Trolley dilemma recruits a structure located in medial part of the prefrontal cortex (the anterior cingulate cortex), while it has been shown that damage to prefrontal regions increases the frequency of utilitarian decisions (Capestany and Harris, 2014).

[16]See also Nahm et al. (2017): *"Large amounts of brain mass and its organic structures, even entire hemispheres, can be drastically altered, damaged, or even absent without causing a substantial impairment of the mental capacities of the affected persons"*. About a patient with hemispherectomy, *"not only does [the patient] perform motor and sensory functions for both sides of the body, [he] performs the associative and intellectual functions normally allocated to two hemispheres"* (Nahm et al., 2017).